Dear Parent:
Your child's love of reading starts here!

Every child learns to read in a different way and at his or her own speed. Some go back and forth between reading levels and read favorite books again and again. Others read through each level in order. You can help your young reader improve and become more confident by encouraging his or her own interests and abilities. From books your child reads with you to the first books he or she reads alone, there are I Can Read Books for every stage of reading:

SHARED READING
Basic language, word repetition, and whimsical illustrations, ideal for sharing with your emergent reader

BEGINNING READING
Short sentences, familiar words, and simple concepts for children eager to read on their own

READING WITH HELP
Engaging stories, longer sentences, and language play for developing readers

READING ALONE
Complex plots, challenging vocabulary, and high-interest topics for the independent reader

ADVANCED READING
Short paragraphs, chapters, and exciting themes for the perfect bridge to chapter books

I Can Read Books have introduced children to the joy of reading since 1957. Featuring award-winning authors and illustrators and a fabulous cast of beloved characters, I Can Read Books set the standard for beginning readers.

A lifetime of discovery begins with the magical words **"I Can Read!"**

Visit www.icanread.com for information
on enriching your child's reading experience.

Pinkalicious®
and the Cupcake Calamity

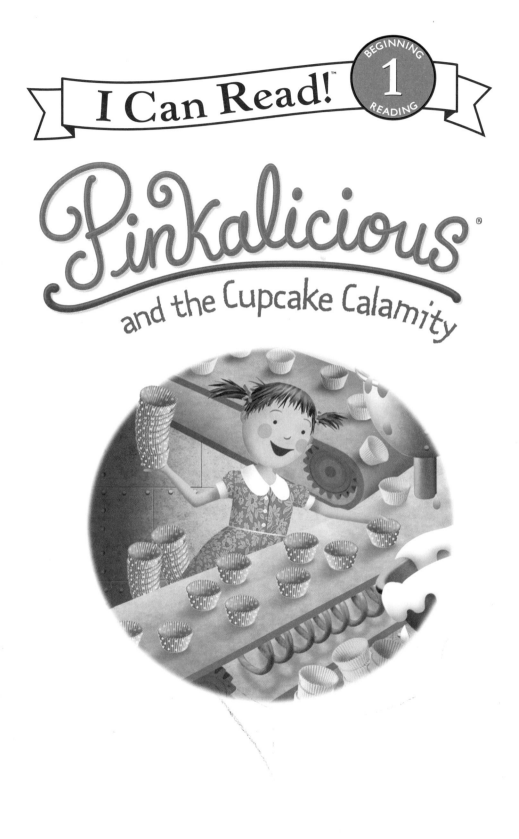

For Sophia

—V.K.

The author gratefully acknowledges
the artistic and editorial contributions
of Robert Masheris and Natalie Engel.

I Can Read Book® is a trademark of HarperCollins Publishers.

Pinkalicious and the Cupcake Calamity
Copyright © 2013 by Victoria Kann

PINKALICIOUS and all related logos and characters are trademarks of Victoria Kann. Used with permission.

Based on the HarperCollins book *Pinkalicious* written by
Victoria Kann and Elizabeth Kann, illustrated by Victoria Kann
All rights reserved. Manufactured in China.
No part of this book may be used or reproduced in any manner whatsoever without
written permission except in the case of brief quotations embodied in critical articles and reviews.
For information address HarperCollins Children's Books, a division of HarperCollins Publishers,
10 East 53rd Street, New York, NY 10022.
www.icanread.com

Library of Congress catalog card number: 2012956496

ISBN 978-0-06-218777-2 (trade bdg.)—ISBN 978-0-06-218776-5 (pbk.)

13 14 15 16 17 SCP 10 9 8 7 6 5 4 3 2 1
❖
First Edition

Pinkalicious®
and the Cupcake Calamity

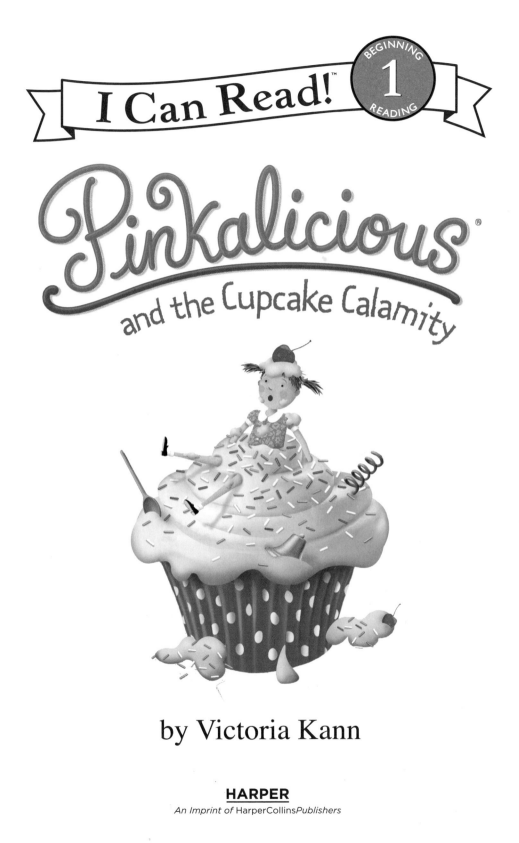

by Victoria Kann

HARPER
An Imprint of HarperCollinsPublishers

One Sunday morning,

we saw a huge crowd outside

Mr. Swizzle's ice cream shop.

I stopped to see what was happening.

"Step right up, folks,"

Mr. Swizzle called.

Behind him was a pink curtain.

"Prepare your taste buds,"
said Mr. Swizzle.
"Dessert is about to be served!"
He lifted the curtain.
The crowd gasped.

Right in front of me was the biggest,

fanciest machine in the world!

Lights were flashing.

Gears were turning.

It hummed, buzzed, and beeped.

"Behold," said Mr. Swizzle,
"my Cupcake-Create-O-Matic!
Just add a dollar and your cupcake
will bake right on the spot!"
I couldn't wait to try it.

BUZZ

HUMM HUMM

BEEP BEEP

Ice Cream

"Me first!" I said.

I ran to the machine

and put in my dollar.

I chose a strawberry cupcake

with pink frosting and pink sprinkles.

I pressed the green button.

Nothing happened.

"Bake!" I said, pressing again.

But no cupcake came out.

"Let me try," said Alison.
One after the other,
people put their money in.
But nothing came out.

"What's going on here?"

The crowd started to grumble.

People were getting upset.

So was I.

I wanted my cupcake!

"I'm so sorry," said Mr. Swizzle.

"Let me get the owner's guide.

I'll have this fixed in a jiffy."

I couldn't wait that long.

I wanted a pink cupcake!

Hmmm . . . I thought.

I looked hard at the machine.

I walked around to the back.

There was a little door
big enough to squeeze through.
So I did!

The Cupcake-Create-O-Matic
was amazing inside!
Mixing bowls whirred
as batter stirred.
Sprinkles and frosting
drizzled everywhere.

I started poking around.

The batter was blending nicely.

It tasted good, too.

There were belts full of
cupcake wrappers,
all ready to be filled.
I swapped out the plain ones
for ones with polka dots.

Then I saw that

only half of the machine

was working.

The mixers weren't pouring batter

into the wrappers.

"There must be a power switch
in here somewhere,"
I said to myself.
I looked up and there it was!

The switch was way up

at the top of the machine.

I climbed all the way there.

"It's cupcake time!" I said

as I flipped it on.

The Cupcake-Create-O-Matic
started rumbling right away.
In fact, it started rattling.
Then, it started shaking.
"Uh-oh," I said.

The machine started filling up
with batter!

"I want to eat a cupcake," I said,

"not BE a cupcake!"

Something was definitely wrong.

The machine shook from side to side.

The walls were starting to crack.

"What is going on?" I cried.

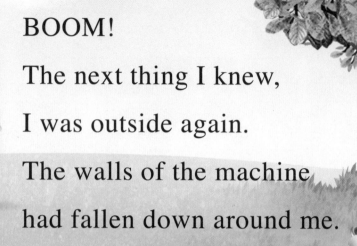

BOOM!

The next thing I knew,

I was outside again.

The walls of the machine

had fallen down around me.

I was sitting on top
of the world's biggest cupcake.

"Pinkalicious!" cried Mr. Swizzle.

"What are you doing up there?

Are you okay?"

I blinked. I smiled.

"Yes. I am perfect!

In fact, I couldn't be better,"

I said.

The crowd roared with laughter.

Mr. Swizzle looked relieved.

"Dig in, everyone!" he said.

Everyone loved the giant treat.

"Sorry about your machine,"
I told Mr. Swizzle.
"That's okay, Pinkalicious," he said.
"From now on, I'll stick to ice cream
and leave the cupcakes to you!"

WE THE PEOPLE

The Declaration of Independence

by Michael Burgan

Content Adviser: Professor Sherry L. Field,
Department of Social Science Education,
College of Education, The University of Georgia

Reading Adviser: Dr. Linda D. Labbo,
Department of Reading Education,
College of Education, The University of Georgia

COMPASS POINT BOOKS

Minneapolis, Minnesota

Compass Point Books
3722 West 50th Street, #115
Minneapolis, MN 55410

Visit Compass Point Books on the Internet at *www.compasspointbooks.com* or e-mail your request
to *custserv@compasspointbooks.com*

Photographs ©: North Wind Picture Archives, cover, 4; Archive Photos, 5, 6, 7; FPG
International/Photoworld, 9; Archive Photos, 10, 12 top and bottom, 13; FPG International, 14;
North Wind Picture Archives, 15; Archive Photos, 16; North Wind Picture Archives, 17, 18, 19;
Archive Photos, 21; Archive Photos/Joe Griffin, 23; North Wind Picture Archives, 24, 27, 28;
Archive Photos, 29, 32; Visuals Unlimited/C.P. George, 33; Archive Photos, 35, 37; North Wind
Picture Archives, 38, 39; Archive Photos, 41.

Editors: E. Russell Primm and Emily J. Dolbear
Photo Researcher: Svetlana Zhurkina
Photo Selector: Dawn Friedman
Design: Bradfordesign, Inc.
Cartography: XNR Productions, Inc.

Library of Congress Cataloging-in-Publication Data

Burgan, Michael.
    The Declaration of Independence / by Michael Burgan.
        p. cm. — (We the people)
    Includes bibliographical references and index.
    Summary: Examines the political situation in America at the time of the troubles between
England and her colonies there and describes how the Declaration of Independence was written
and accepted.
    ISBN 0-7565-0042-7
    1. United States. Declaration of Independence—Juvenile literature. 2. United States—
Politics and government—1775–1783—Juvenile literature. [1. United States. Declaration of
Independence. 2. United States—Politics and government—1775–1783.] I. Title. II. We the
people (Compass Point Books).
    E221 .B945 2000
    973.3'13—dc21   00-008671

TABLE OF CONTENTS

A Decision about Independence

On June 7, 1776, members, or delegates, from the thirteen American **colonies** gathered in Philadelphia. They met at the Pennsylvania State House (now Independence Hall).

These men formed the Second Continental

Independence Hall in Philadelphia

Congress. The colonies were rebelling against Britain and its king, George III. The Congress now had to decide whether America should declare its independence. It was a very important decision.

George Washington in 1775

Fighting between the colonists and British troops broke out in April 1775 in Massachusetts. The Continental Congress then named General George Washington commander of the American troops. His soldiers had already won the Battle of Bunker Hill.

The British had held off an American raid in Canada and were now preparing for an attack along America's East Coast. And spies in London, England, had learned that King George had hired foreign troops to fight in America.

The delegates of the Continental Congress discussed their next step. The colonists had mixed feelings about declaring independence from Britain. About one-third of the American people wanted independence. About one-third believed the

The delegates of the Continental Congress

colonies should remain under British rule. The rest couldn't make up their minds.

The delegates in Philadelphia were also unsure, but they knew time was running out. They had to make the decision.

Richard Henry Lee

Richard Henry Lee of Virginia rose and addressed the Congress. He presented a **resolution**, or statement. It said, "that these united colonies are, and of right ought to be, free and independent states." Within a month, the Continental Congress finally made its decision. It approved one of the world's most important political documents—the Declaration of Independence.

Map of the British colonies

DEEP ROOTS OF THE STRUGGLE

Before 1763, most colonists were proud to call themselves British. The settlers who had crossed the Atlantic Ocean had brought their political and social traditions with them. They believed the British government, or **Parliament,** was the best in

American colonists held town meetings in public buildings such as Faneuil Hall in Boston.

9

the world. They also had developed new freedoms in America.

Colonists burned printed matter to protest the Stamp Act.

But things changed after the British won the French and Indian War (1756–1763). Although the British had driven the French out of North America, the victory had been expensive. In the future, Parliament said, the American colonies would have to pay more money for the troops that defended them. That money would come from taxes.

The most unpopular new tax law was the Stamp Act, passed in 1765. Every piece of printed material sold in America, including books, newspapers, wills, and playing cards, would be taxed. The Americans quickly protested the Stamp Act.

Few people enjoy paying taxes. But the Americans thought they had a good reason to complain. In Britain, people voted for their representatives in Parliament. These representatives defended the interests of the people who elected them. The Americans had no elected representatives in Parliament, however. The British government was passing tax laws on Americans who had no say in the matter.

Parliament stopped the tax on paper goods. But its leaders refused to give up the right to collect other taxes. It continued to pass new taxes and other laws that limited American freedoms.

11

TROUBLES IN BOSTON

The colonists who strongly opposed the taxes were sometimes called **Patriots**. Boston, Massachusetts, was one of the centers of Patriot activity. The Patriot leaders there included Samuel Adams and his cousin, John Adams.

Samuel Adams

At times, the protests became violent so the British government put troops in Boston to keep order. Seeing these soldiers, called **redcoats**, only made people even angrier.

John Adams

12

The Boston Massacre

Patriots disguised as Indians throw tea into Boston Harbor.

In 1770, a local mob clashed with some soldiers. The redcoats fired their guns and killed five people. This event became known as the Boston Massacre.

Bad feelings between the Bostonians and the British grew worse. In 1773, the Patriots decided to protest against the tax on tea. They raided three ships carrying tea in Boston Harbor. The angry

Patriots threw thousands of pounds of the tea into the water. The Boston Tea Party was the first real act of rebellion.

The British Parliament responded with tougher laws. Britain ordered all the colonies to allow British troops to live in houses, inns, and

Colonists were forced to allow British soldiers to live in their homes.

15

Delegates of the First Continental Congress discuss the issues.

other buildings. More colonists now thought Parliament and King George had gone too far. In September 1774, representatives from the colonies met in Philadelphia at the First Continental Congress to talk about these problems.

THE FIRST CONTINENTAL CONGRESS

In 1775, Paul Revere rode through the night to warn colonists that British troops were coming.

Some delegates at the Congress did not want to break off their ties with Britain. George Galloway of Pennsylvania wrote a resolution saying that the Americans were "faithful subjects" of King George. The resolution failed to pass, but still only a few delegates supported American independence.

The First Continental Congress finally decided that the colonies would cut off all trade with Great Britain unless it ended the tax laws. The representatives also agreed to meet again if another crisis arose. That time came just a few months later—in the spring of 1775.

BATTLES AT LEXINGTON AND CONCORD

For the British, Massachusetts was the chief trouble spot. In April 1775, British soldiers were sent to destroy supplies and weapons the colonists had stored for their defense. The soldiers marched from Boston into the countryside. Along the way, they ran into armed colonists. These Massachusetts

A minuteman prepares for battle.

18

In 1775, war broke out between the colonists and the British.

soldiers were called **minutemen**. They got their name because they were supposed to be ready to grab their guns and fight at a moment's notice.

Captain John Parker led a group of minutemen in the town of Lexington. As the redcoats approached, he told his troops "Don't fire unless fired upon, but if they mean to have a war, let it begin here." And so it did.

No one knows who fired the first shot. The minutemen and redcoats exchanged fire in Lexington, and then in the nearby town of Concord. By the end of the day, seventy-three British soldiers and forty-nine colonists were dead.

Massachusetts was in rebellion and the other colonies soon joined it. Another Continental Congress was called to meet in Philadelphia.

THE SECOND CONTINENTAL CONGRESS

Thomas Paine

After the battles at Lexington and Concord, the fighting increased. King George stood firm against the colonies. He refused to give in to their demands. As the Second Continental Congress debated what to do, the colonists began to turn against Great Britain.

In January 1776, a small book called *Common Sense* went on sale in Philadelphia. Its author was Thomas Paine. After arriving from England in 1774, he supported the cause of independence.

21

In *Common Sense*, he spelled out why all Americans should break away from Great Britain.

Paine wrote that King George was a "royal brute [or beast]." He also said that America would achieve greatness only as an independent nation. Paine wrote in a simple style that any reader could understand. *Common Sense* quickly sold more than 100,000 copies. It helped boost the call for independence.

By June 1776, the Second Continental Congress was almost ready to take action. Richard Henry Lee offered his resolution in favor of independence. But some representatives were not ready to vote on it. Some delegates still needed instructions from the leaders of their colonies.

To give members more time, the Congress decided to put off the vote on independence for

COMMON SENSE;

ADDRESSED TO THE

INHABITANTS

OF

AMERICA,

On the following interesting

SUBJECTS.

I. Of the Origin and Design of Government in general, with concise Remarks on the English Constitution.

II. Of Monarchy and Hereditary Succession.

III. Thoughts on the present State of American Affairs.

IV. Of the present Ability of America, with some miscellaneous Reflections.

Man knows no Master save creating HEAVEN,
Or those whom choice and common good ordain.
THOMSON.

PHILADELPHIA;

Printed, and Sold, by R. BELL, in Third-Street,

MDCCLXXVI.

Thomas Paine argued for independence in his book Common Sense.

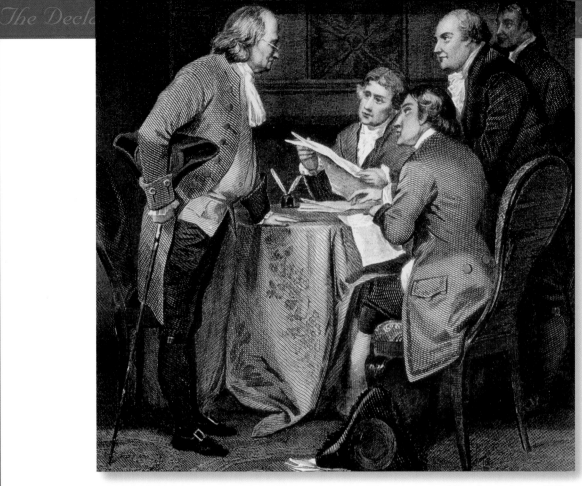

The Committee of Five

three weeks. During that time, they would choose
a committee to write a document. If the Congress
voted for Lee's resolution, this document would
explain to the world why America was declaring
its independence.

The committee had five members: Roger Sherman of Connecticut, John Adams of Massachusetts, Robert Livingston of New York, Pennsylvania's Benjamin Franklin, and a tall Virginian named Thomas Jefferson. They were called the Committee of Five.

When they met, they asked Jefferson to be the main author of the **declaration**. "Mr. Jefferson," said John Adams, "had the reputation of a masterly pen."

In addition to his writing skills, Jefferson was a strong believer in independence. Adams also thought it was helpful that Jefferson was from the South. The British would see that all Americans, not only the rebels of Massachusetts, supported independence.

WRITING THE DECLARATION

At thirty-three, Thomas Jefferson was one of the youngest delegates at the Second Continental Congress. He was a **scholar** with an interest in arts and sciences as well as politics.

Jefferson wrote his declaration in a rented room. He usually worked standing up and sometimes he worked late into the night. Jefferson also showed his writings to Adams and Franklin. They scribbled notes on the pages and Jefferson added their comments.

Jefferson once said that no one book influenced what he wrote in the declaration. But historians have noted connections between specific writings and Jefferson's work.

Thomas Jefferson writing the Declaration of Independence

27

A draft of the declaration in Thomas Jefferson's handwriting

Another Virginia politician, George Mason, had just written the Virginia Declaration of Rights. Mason said "that all men are by nature free and independent and have certain . . . rights." An earlier British scholar named John Locke influenced both Mason and Jefferson.

George Mason

In his writings, Locke had discussed the idea of natural laws. According to Locke, these laws, created by God, affect every human being, and every human knows they are true. No one, not

29

even kings, can break these natural laws. Jefferson wrote about natural laws as he drew up the declaration.

On June 28, 1776, the Committee of Five gave Jefferson's work to the Second Continental Congress. The Congress, however, was still not ready to vote. Delegates from Maryland and New York were still waiting to hear from their leaders whether they could vote for independence. The first debate on Jefferson's declaration was put off until July 1.

THE VOTE FOR INDEPENDENCE

When the Continental Congress met again, it got some bad news. Dozens of British ships were now near the coast of New York City. In Charleston, South Carolina, fifty-three British ships patrolled the waters. The delegates faced the threat of an even deadlier war. At the same time, they met to consider Jefferson's declaration and the vote for independence.

The debate that day bored John Adams. What was said "had been repeated . . . in that room before a hundred times, for six months past," he later said. One delegate, however, woke everyone up. John Dickinson of Pennsylvania spoke strongly against independence. "I know the name of liberty is dear

John Dickinson of Pennsylvania spoke against independence.

to each one of us," Dickinson said. "But have we not enjoyed liberty even under the English?"

Adams then stood up to challenge Dickinson. He noted that King George had already said he would not defend the American colonies from outside attack. So Americans were in many ways independent already. Although there is no record of Adams's exact words, Jefferson said that they had "a power that moved us from our seats."

Delegates to the Continental Congress met in this room.

After Adams sat down, the delegates took
a first vote for independence. Nine colonies voted
for it. South Carolina and Pennsylvania voted
against it. Delaware had two delegates—one
voted for and one voted against. The New York
delegates were still waiting for instruction. So the

Congress delayed a final vote for one more day.

This time, on July 2, 1776, the vote for independence was clear. South Carolina and Pennsylvania switched their votes. Though he was dying from cancer, Caesar Rodney, Delaware's third delegate, rode his horse nonstop through the night to break the tie in favor of independence. The New York delegates, who still had not heard from their leaders, did not vote. With the issue of independence finally settled, the Congress turned to Jefferson's declaration.

FINISHING JEFFERSON'S WORK

Jefferson had divided his document into three sections. The first section was a preamble, or introduction. The second included a list of America's complaints against King George. The last part was the Declaration of American Independence. For the first time, the name *United States of America* appeared in a government document.

This famous painting by John Trumbull shows the signers of the Declaration of Independence.

35

Today, most Americans know the preamble. Jefferson's most famous lines come in the second paragraph: "We hold these truths to be **self-evident**, that all men are created equal, that they are **endowed** by their Creator with certain **unalienable** Rights, that among these are Life, Liberty and the pursuit of Happiness."

Not all the words in the final version were exactly what Jefferson wrote. The Committee of Five had made some changes. And the Continental Congress spent a few days making its own changes. Some parts that might have offended British citizens were taken out. So was a mention of slavery. Finally, on July 4, 1776, the Congress approved the Declaration of Independence.

The signatures on the Declaration of the Independence

John Hancock, the president of the Congress, signed the declaration. The rest of the delegates later signed another copy of the document.

Celebrating Independence

The original Declaration of Independence went to a printer. Copies were then sent to all thirteen colonies. The declaration was first publicly read on July 8, 1776. In Philadelphia, John Adams said a festive crowd came to hear the news, and "the bells rang all day and almost all night." Across

The Declaration of Independence is read to the crowds.

Tearing down the statue of King George in New York City

America, people cheered whenever the document was read.

In New York City, when a crowd heard the Declaration of Independence, they knocked down a nearby statue of King George. The metal from the statue was later turned into bullets for General Washington's army.

When the celebrations ended, Americans were citizens of a new country—the United States of America. They knew plenty of hard work remained to be done.

The Continental Congress was now the government of a new nation. It had to try to win help from powerful countries, such as France. It also had to make sure Washington had an army strong enough to fight the British. A long war lay ahead.

During the debates on the declaration, John Adams had written a letter to his wife Abigail. His words expressed what many Americans must have felt after hearing the Declaration of Independence. "I am well aware," he wrote, "of the [work], and blood, and treasure, that it will cost us to maintain this declaration, and support and defend these states. Yet, through all the gloom, I can see the rays of ravishing light and glory."

The original Declaration of Independence is on display in Washington, D.C.

GLOSSARY

colonies—the thirteen British territories that became the United States of America

declaration—an announcement

endowed—given

minutemen—colonists who were ready to grab their guns at a moment's notice

Parliament—the British government

Patriots—American colonists who wanted independence from Britain

redcoats—British soldiers, named after the color of their uniforms

resolution—a statement

scholar—an intellectual, a person who loves learning

self-evident—plain, clear

unalienable—not to be taken away

DID YOU KNOW?

- The basement of Independence Hall was once Philadelphia's dog pound.

- Like other documents of the time, the Declaration of Independence was probably rolled up for storage.

- In 1941, after the Japanese attack on Pearl Harbor, Hawaii, the original Declaration of Independence was moved to a vault in Fort Knox.

- At the National Archives Building in Washington, D.C., the Declaration of Independence is kept in an upright glass and plastic case that has been tested with firearms. It is moved to an underground vault at night.

IMPORTANT DATES

Timeline

1763   Britain defeats France in the French and Indian War.

1765   Parliament passes the Stamp Act, which taxes colonists on all printed items.

1770   Five colonists are killed in the Boston Massacre on March 5.

1773   The Boston Tea Party takes place on December 16.

1774   The First Continental Congress meets in Philadelphia in September.

1775   Lexington and Concord battles take place between Massachusetts minutemen and British troops in April.

1776   The Second Continental Congress meets in Philadelphia on June 7; the Congress votes for independence on July 2 and the Congress approves the declaration on July 4; the declaration is first publicly read on July 8.

IMPORTANT PEOPLE

JOHN ADAMS
(1735–1826), *delegate from Massachusetts, second U.S. president (1797–1801)*

SAMUEL ADAMS
(1722–1803), *leader of the Patriots*

BENJAMIN FRANKLIN
(1706–1790), *delegate from Pennsylvania*

JOHN HANCOCK
(1737–1793), *president of the Continental Congress*

THOMAS JEFFERSON
(1743–1826), *delegate from Virginia at the Continental Congress and author of the Declaration of Independence, third U.S. president from (1801–1809)*

THOMAS PAINE
(1737–1809), *author of Common Sense and other political books*

GEORGE WASHINGTON
(1732–1799), *American general, served as first U.S. president from 1789 to 1797*

WANT TO KNOW MORE?

At the Library

Brenner, Barbara. *If You Were There in 1776.* New York: Simon & Schuster Books for Young Readers, 1994.

Fisher, Dorothy Canfield. *Our Independence and the Constitution.* New York: Random House, 1987.

Harness, Cheryl. *Young John Quincy.* New York: Bradbury Press, 1994.

Quiri, Patricia Ryon. *The Declaration of Independence.* Danbury, Conn.: Children's Press, 1998.

On the Web

The Declaration of Independence

http://www.law.indiana.edu/uslawdocs/declaration.html

For a complete text of the document and a list of all the signers

Declaring Independence: Drafting the Documents

http://lcweb.loc.gov/exhibits/declara/declara1.htm

For a chronology of events leading to the creation of the document

The History Place: American Revolution

http://www.historyplace.com/unitedstates/revolution/index.html

For a complete chronology of the Revolutionary War

Through the Mail

National Archives and Records Administration

700 Pennsylvania Avenue, N.W.

Washington, DC 20408

To find out more about the original Declaration of Independence

On the Road

Independence National Historical Park

Visitor Center

3rd and Chestnut Streets

Philadelphia, PA 19106

215/597-8974

To visit where the Declaration of Independence was signed

INDEX

About the Author

Michael Burgan is a freelance writer for both children and adults.
A history graduate of the University of Connecticut, he has written
more than thirty fiction and nonfiction children's books for various
publishers. For adult audiences, he has written news articles, essays,
and plays. Michael Burgan is a recipient of an Edpress Award and
belongs to the Society of Children's Book Writers and Illustrators.

48